My New York: City Poems

By

Betty Farber

Houts & Home Publications LLC

Maryville, Missouri

*Dedicated to the members of
the Poets' Workshop at Quest
for encouraging me to
print a book of
my New York City poems.*

Cover photo: Emily M. Bush
Interior layout design: Amy Houts/Megg Houts
Cover Design: Megg Houts

© 2015 by Betty Farber
All rights reserved. No part of this publication may be reproduced, stored in retrieval systems, or transmitted in any form or by any means, electronic, photocopying, mechanical, recording, or otherwise, without prior written permission of Betty Farber or
Houts & Home Publications LLC.

Printed in the United States of America
ISBN 978-0-9855084-3-2

For inquiries contact:
Amy Houts, President, Houts & Home Publications LLC
Telephone: 660.562.3122
Email: houtsandhome@gmail.com
Website: www.houtsandhome.com

Library of Congress Control Number: 2014960090

TABLE OF CONTENTS

Moving to Manhattan	8
Enchanted April	9
City Flowers	10
Butterfly in the City	11
Let Us Go…	12
Elephant Graveyard	13
Winter Weather	14
Everyday Bravery	15
Living Well	16
At the New York Philharmonic	17
Old Age	18
Rehearsal	20
The Play's the Thing	21
Subway Suspense	22
Subway Surprises	23
Superwoman	24
Surka's Stories	25
Help Wanted	26
Inspiration	27
Childhood Fantasy	28
State Fair	29
I Don't Want to Move	30
Tree at My New Window	31

Abundance	32
Barbarian Invasion	33
Starbucks Times Two	34
Shopping at Lord & Taylor	36
Dreams	37
Bagels and Romance	38
Advice for Troubled Times	39
Walking Companions	40
A Polite Protest by a New Yorker	41
Communication	42
Southern Discomfort	44
Two Proposals	45
I Hear a Poem	46
Night Sounds	47
Brief Encounter	48
Foolish Things	50
Echoes	51
Published in Q Review	52

MOVING TO MANHATTAN
FROM THE EAST END OF LONG ISLAND

When we were planning our relocation,
Our neighbors indulged in speculation
As to how we would handle the situation.
Would we feel angst and desolation?
They worried about the separation
From friends — the complex navigation
Of various means of transportation
Resulting in feelings of consternation.

Overcome with irritation
And filled with righteous indignation,
We tired of their recitations
Of City trials and tribulations.

And here are the happy revelations:
Despite their dreary expectations
We thrived in this place of fascination.
We tell them with joy and jubilation
If THEY want to try a new location,
Call on us for a consultation.

ENCHANTED APRIL

On a city street lined with pear trees,
An April breeze ruffles the branches.
Countless pear blossoms fall quietly
Like snowflakes.

  As I stare in wonder,
West 25th Street becomes a fairyland.
Do I alone sense the magic?
No...

  A slender young Asian girl
Rises in the air to catch a blossom
And having her prize in hand
  Turns to smile at me.

CITY FLOWERS

Walking past dusty trees, on West 28th Street,
Striding quickly along dirty sidewalks
Teeming with people hurrying to work,
Ignoring store windows with FOR RENT signs...
I find myself against all expectation
      In an English garden.
Green tubs of fir trees line the street.
Pots of flowers: marigolds, begonias, tulips,
Daffodils on both sides of my path.
      Shop owners
Keep a wary eye on their prized blossoms.
Newly watered, they fill the air with aromas
Unfamiliar to city streets. The duality
Of life in Manhattan brings a smile,
      And my heart dances.

BUTTERFLY IN THE CITY

A teenager crosses East 61st Street
With a white butterfly
Circling around his head.

He opens his hand
Palm up, not to catch it
But to give the creature
A large landing field.

A white-haired lady
Crossing alongside him
Notices the butterfly
And smiles at a memory,
"Yesterday, one landed on my shoulder
and stayed there for an hour."

They both smile in shared wonder
At the city's surprises.

LET US GO...

Let us go then, you and I
To England, Wales, or the Isle of Skye
To Greece and Turkey to drink and dance
To Germany, Italy, Spain and France.
Denmark, Norway and Sweden are cool.
Let's go to a village in Greenland called "Thule."
Or fly to the Southern Hemisphere.
It's winter there, when it's summer here.

I love where I live, so please don't have pity.
But save me from August in New York City!

ELEPHANT GRAVEYARD

I was familiar with elephant graveyards —
Having seen them in old Tarzan movies —
Carcasses and tusks strewn here and there
With abandon in a jungle clearing
Where elephants go to die.

Thought again of those graveyards, after the storm
As I wandered on rain-drenched city streets —
Carcasses of umbrellas with ribs like tusks
Useless, abandoned, their lives at an end,
Strewn on the sidewalks along East Sixty-First Street.

WINTER WEATHER

Snowstorms keep battering us;
The icy sidewalks dare me to plant my feet
On their slippery surface. Mounds of the white stuff
Keep me separated from the bus that will take me home.

Home where it is warm, where I can heat a cup
Of dark cocoa topped with mini-marshmallows…
Walking home from the bus stop, icy pitfalls everywhere,
A woman offers me her arm — angel in a fur-lined hoodie.

EVERYDAY BRAVERY

You must be brave to climb a subway stair
Slushy with snow that salt does not erase,
Or walk half-empty twilight streets, aware
That one behind you will not show his face.
You must be strong to walk on wintry roads
On ice that's slippery and smooth as glass.
Your final trace of bravery erodes
Waiting for the gusts of wind to pass.
You need a hero's courage when your key
Opens the door of your dark rooms alone
Or when you read a bloody mystery
Sure that you hear next door a chilling moan.
And you must be a valiant poet indeed
To clutch your heart and hold your every breath
And take your pen in hand to fill the need
To write a poem that scares you half to death.

LIVING WELL

I see the best of the Broadway shows
(with discount tickets from TDF).
I dine in Manhattan eateries
(when Restaurant Week offers prix fixe meals).
I shop in posh Fifth Avenue stores
(when they advertise enormous sales).
I travel everywhere in the world
(when my frequent-flyer miles add up).

I don't regret not being rich:
Living well is the best revenge.

AT THE NEW YORK PHILHARMONIC

Seated directly in front of me — a teenaged couple.
From the backs of their heads I observe that the boy is tall,
With jet-black hair hanging neatly to his shoulders.
The girl with a blondish chignon, several strands undone,
Shoulders bare in the air-conditioned hall.
The first movement of the symphony begins.
She lays her head upon his shoulder,
Nestling against his neck.
He sits upright, looking straight ahead,
Not resting his head against hers, not turning to smile,
Until she sits again straight in her seat.
A dozen times, through all four movements,
This sad pas de deux is repeated,
Her head on his shoulder, his body unresponding.
When the music ends, he shows what flames his passion:
Applauding loudly, shouting "Bravo, Bravo!"
Her passion is for him. His, for the music.
What will become of this romance?
Can love blossom in such circumstance?
Perhaps.
       Perhaps not.

OLD AGE

Definition: Fey: (adjective) slightly insane; suggestive of an elf in strangeness and otherworldliness

What does old age look like?
Is it curious, vital, eager to learn?
Is it quiet, thoughtful,
Wondering about tomorrow?
Is it fey, whimsical, off-the wall?

Standing in line
To attend a concert at Carnegie Hall,
I met a well-dressed, elderly lady,
Whose conversation seemed to me
Both original and strange.
"What does the word 'soon' mean?" she asked.
"Why do you want to know?" I wondered.
"They just said that the theater will open soon."
"I guess it means
Whatever you want it to mean," I replied.
She seemed satisfied.

A minute later, still on line behind me, she boldly asked,
"Will you lend me some money?"
Startled, I laughed. She didn't join in.
"Sorry. I thought you were joking," I replied,
"Why do you need money?" She opened a magazine.
"I want to buy this house in Montana."
"I don't have money for a house in Montana," said I.

Was she demented, or making conversation?
Was it silly or whimsical, or just talk?
Or does old age give you permission
To be slightly insane?

REHEARSAL

In my meditation session
Our teacher revealed
That monks try to simulate dying
To understand how it would feel
To endure this ultimate experience.
I have tried to replicate their endeavors
In my leather chair in a deep sleep.
I failed. I could not pretend to die
Or even imagine Heaven.

But when I was in a crowded cafe
Attached to an off-Broadway theater
With music screaming in my ears
And people squeezed like lemons,
Talking at the top of their lungs
It was like a hint of Hell.
Then doors opened for me
And the usher took my ticket.
Finally, I was able to enter
The Heavenly peace of the theater.

THE PLAY'S THE THING

I'm so stuffed with emotion I can hardly contain
The tingling excitement that inhabits my brain.
As I wait for the time when the lights start to dim
And the curtain goes up, I am filled to the brim
With wonder about the magic to come.
Will the scene be a mansion or a ghetto-like slum?
What stories? What Insights? What hopes and what fears?
Will I be inspired? Will it move me to tears?
Will the playwright be seen as another O'Neill?
Will the actors amaze with portrayals so real?

Or, despite my playgoer's intuition,
If the playwright has offered a poor submission,
Will I be leaving at intermission?

SUBWAY SUSPENSE

After a long ride uptown from Rector Street
Ending in the station at Lexington and 59th
My heart stops in suspense.
What awaits me at the Exit?

My eyes seek the UP escalator.
Is it moving? Or are the people moving
While the escalator stands still?
I take a deep breath and start to climb

One two three four flights.
And that's not the end of my getaway
From the dark subway station.
Two more flights before I escape.

Heart pumping, gasping for breath
I reach the street, grateful for daylight.
The next morning, more thrills await!
The DOWN escalator doesn't work either.

SUBWAY SURPRISES

Daily concerts from musicians,
Singing gospel music, playing guitars,
Holding out a shopping bag for coins,
Leaving the train at the next stop.
No surprise.

Yesterday a drummer sat nearby,
Practicing his craft: tap tap taptaptap,
Earphones feeding him the music,
Rising to go without asking for a dime.
Surprise.

"One Man Show!" shouted a youth.
Opened his backpack, took out a CD player.
Music blared, too loud for comfort.
He suddenly said, "No One Man Show," and left.
Surprise.

Commotion — a violent voice.
"You wanna get hurt?" Passengers panic.
Woman begs, "Please. Wait for the train to stop."
"I apologize," a man shouts to the crowd.
"Thank you," says another man's voice.
"Don't thank me! I just apologize," he growls.
BIG surprise.

SUPERWOMAN

Long black hair billowing behind her,
A floor-length purple cloak on her back
That floats to reveal black high-heeled shoes,
She runs past me on 61st Street.

Is she rushing to catch the Third Avenue bus?
Or late for the R train to wake up Wall Street?
A glance at her face will give me a clue.
I turn the corner. She is gone.

No bus has arrived. Subway stairs — empty.
Is she flying above the traffic on Third Avenue,
Purple cloak lifting her aloft? Look! Up in the sky!
A purple light shines in the misty morning.

SURKA'S STORIES

My mother told us
Stories about Russia
Where she lived as a child.
How she crept from her house
To a gypsy encampment
Listening to music
And dancing with gypsies.

Her name was Surka
(Sarah in English).
A Romany man
Said she was one of them.
"Your mother has fair hair
But you are dark, like a gypsy.
You were stolen from us
When you were a baby."
She ran home in fear
And never returned
To dance with the gypsies.

My mother's great grandchild,
Theatrical Sarah,
Delights in dancing,
And calls herself Surka
When she performs.
And what is the nickname
For dancers on Broadway
Who perform for the love of it?
They are called "Gypsies!"

HELP WANTED

My mother left school at thirteen,
Wrapped her braids around her head,
And went to work for a milliner.
She didn't have working papers,
So when the inspector came,
They hid her in a storeroom.

At eighteen, she applied for a job
At Metropolitan Life Insurance Company.
"We don't hire Jewish girls," they told her,
But the manager said, "I'll give you a try."
And they liked her work so well
They asked her to recommend a friend.
"I have a cousin who's a good worker,
But she's Jewish too," said my mother.
And that's how she broke down barriers
At the Brooklyn office of Met Life.

INSPIRATION

On the balcony of a cruise ship, I saw
A vision, rising gracefully out of the fog:
Lady Liberty blessing New York Harbor,
A shadowy grey, with her lamp shining brightly.
Is that how she looked a hundred years ago
When a little Russian girl, hugging the smokestack
Of a different ship, gazed at her?
                            "An inspiration to us all,"
I used to say. Not speaking of the statue,
But of that little Russian girl who lit my way.

CHILDHOOD FANTASY

Floating out of the Brooklyn Public library,
A rainbow of fairy tales in my book bag,
A book open in front of me, I drift
Down East 13th Street.

Tangled forests grow on the Brooklyn streets
Hiding castles where sleeping maidens lie.
As I cross Avenue O, trumpets sound
"Long live the queen!"

Ogres pursue me up the stairs
Until with a golden key I unlock the door
And find a haven on the couch
Where I can read happily ever after.

STATE FAIR

On a winter's night in 2011
I watched a movie made in 1945
In technicolor bright as a lollipop.

Jeanne Crain sat in the window
Of her Iowa farmhouse
In the heat of a summer's day
And sang, "It Might As Well Be Spring."

I was fourteen years old in 1945
Looking out on clotheslines
From the window of my Brooklyn apartment,
Feeling restless and flowing in the wind.

Sixty-five years later, I can remember how it felt
To be fourteen and looking for love.
The miracle was that I found it
And it will always be with me.

That's even better than a Hollywood ending.

I DON'T WANT TO MOVE

I Don't Want to Move.
I've lived in Manhattan, Brooklyn and Queens,
Nassau and Suffolk Counties,
St. Louis, Missouri and Memphis, Tennessee,
And I Don't Want to Move.

I Don't Want to Move.
Grew up in a three-room walkup,
Rattled around in a seven-room ranch,
Felt cozy in a five-room colonial,
Rented a split-level monster,
Enjoyed a doorman-guarded condo,
And I Don't Want to Move.

I Don't Want to Move.
I've had homes with attics and basements,
Garages and outdoor decks,
A home office with a bay window,
A sunroom overlooking a garden,
And I Don't Want to Move.

Oh, well. There's the van.
Careful with that lamp!
It belonged to my mother....

TREE AT MY NEW WINDOW

I cannot draw my curtain open —
A bed sheet, taped to the window.
A different window and a different view...
No balconied buildings now,
No buses and taxis, traversing the street.

There is a tree outside this window,
My new green view of the world.
At night the tree is backlit by the street lamp —
The bed sheet morphs into a silver screen,
Projecting the leaves' shadows on my vision.
In calm weather, the branches move slowly, gracefully.
In a storm they lurch crazily back and forth, lunging at me,
Then pulling away, monstrously growling thunder.
I welcome my window tree, and I am not afraid.

ABUNDANCE

When they talk of abundance in New York City,
They mean an abundance of wealth,
Of people, of cars and buses,
Noise and confusion.

But do they know about
The branches of a city pear tree
Pushing up against my window
Filling every inch of my view
With exuberant young blossoms?

BARBARIAN INVASION

Pushing, laughing, shouting,
Staring, shoving, demanding,
They invade the subway car.
After a day's pillaging in Central Park,
Wearing t-shirts, shorts, backpacks,
Day-camp name printed bright blue,
They take over the train.

Their demands are extreme:
They want our attention, approval, applause.
Fearless and vulnerable,
They live life with ceaseless energy.

Subway riders frown
Or just look bored
At the end of a weary day.

One small barbarian
Wanders among the passengers.
Choosing the empty seat next to mine,
Her dark head settles on my shoulder,
And I am converted to her cause.

STARBUCKS TIMES TWO

At the corner Starbucks
On Columbus Avenue,
Had my morning coffee
With a crispy croissant.
Unfinished coffee
Dropped on the floor!
Wiped up with napkins
Helped by a worker
"No problem," said she.

A different Starbucks
For my afternoon meal.
(It's just so convenient.
When I'm much too early
For today's matinee.)
A French-speaking father
And his ten-year-old son
Sit at the next table,
Chatting in French,
And drinking hot chocolate.
Boy drops his hot chocolate
On table and floor!
I hand him my napkin.

Angry-faced father
Grabs bunches of napkins
To wipe up the mess.
I think, "Please don't feel bad.
I did the same thing
Early this morning

In a different Starbucks."
Would that revelation
Be a real comfort?
I never will know.
I do not speak French.

In my next incarnation
I will know every language,
So if someone is careless
And drops his hot chocolate
I will know what kind words
Will make it all right.

SHOPPING AT LORD & TAYLOR

I look for beautiful clothes at a bargain price.
GREAT SALES! 70% OFF, say the ads
So what's this on the jacket's price tag?
Seven hundred and seventeen dollars.
Nice alliteration. Outrageous price.
Look instead at tee shirts: here's a pretty pink one –
Sixty-five dollars. Oh. That one's not ON SALE.
I'll look for bedroom slippers.
How much can bedroom slippers cost?
I go to the eighth floor lingerie.
"We don't carry bedroom slippers any more!
You could try J.C. Penney. But they're not in New York City."
That's when I feel that I'm in a waking dream
Where all I experience is confusion and frustration.
Down to the first floor where an elegant necklace
 Is hanging out in the open, for any thief
To lift and take away, price $155.00.
I picture myself walking down Fifth Avenue in a new hat.
Reality goes out the revolving doors when I try on
A little straw fedora costing $238.
Why are the numbers familiar?
My public school in Brooklyn was number 238.
It can't be the price of a hat!

I walk out.

Up Fifth Avenue to 42nd Street. Am I hallucinating?
I'm not sure of the answer until the M104 bus stops
In the real world and takes me home.
I don't even think about the price.

DREAMS

I put my arms through the sleeves
Of the apple-green jacket,
Feel the soft wool glide
Over my upper body
Like waves on a bay beach,
Gently caressing me.
I am Cinderella being dressed
In a gown of pure moonlight
By her fairy godmother.
All my dreams are woven
Into that designer jacket —
Dreams of travel around the world
Owning a painting by Mary Cassatt
Seeing Broadway shows
From the third row orchestra.
But even at half price
It is too much to pay
For an apple-green dream.
So I coldly remove the jacket
And hang it on its hanger.
But I might look again
In a few more weeks.

Or I might take a trip around the world.

BAGELS AND ROMANCE

Bagelworks on First Avenue
Sells a variety of bagels
To please anyone's taste.
I'm waiting for my order to be filled.

A woman behind me is talking
On a cell phone to her boyfriend.
"I'm at Bagelworks right now.
What kind of bagel do you want:
Sesame, whole wheat, pumpernickel
Sourdough, poppy seed, everything?
What? A plain bagel?" She is incredulous
And complains to the nearest stranger,
"I thought he was unique, unconventional,
 And he orders a plain bagel. I may
Have to rethink this relationship."

"That man is in deep trouble," I say to myself,
As I pay for my bagel order.
With an eye on my own relationships
I take home sesame, sourdough, everything.

ADVICE FOR TROUBLED TIMES

In this time of bleak recession
How to fight against depression?
You'll have no bank account Hereafter
The only thing to save is laughter.
The lack of stocks or bonds or money
Seems minor when your friends are funny.
Can't fund your yearly trip to Crete?
Stretch your legs on a New York street.
Get some inexpensive thrills
In Riverdale or Forest Hills.
When you read the New York Times
And you weep at all the crimes,
Take a page from Scarlett's book.
Though you feel you are forsook,
Don't be killed with pain and sorrow —
Smile and shelve it 'til tomorrow.

WALKING COMPANIONS

My daughter walks
With a friend each day.
I have no friends
Who love to take long walks.
So I walk alone,
Watching the dog walkers expertly
Leading on leashes three or four canines,
Large, small, many different breeds:
Beagles, collies and spaniels
Walking quietly, contentedly
On city streets with their dog walker.

Could there be a people walker
For folks like me without companions?
Couldn't we benefit from the friendship
Of three or four folks large and small,
Many different ethnicities?
I'm sure we would walk quietly, contentedly,
Getting acquainted with each other,
Enjoying the rich friendships
That develop as we meander
Down the city streets.

A POLITE PROTEST BY A NEW YORKER

(TRAVEL+LEISURE Poll: New York Voted Rudest City in the U.S.A.)

When you think of rudeness, don't think of us —
I am given a seat on the subway or bus.
Riding calmly through traffic, I'm satisfied
When folks thank the driver for their ride.

In the subway, a MetroCard machine
Made me feel grim and a little green,
But I had to buy one for a guest.
A young man saw my urgent request.
As a New York City Samaritan
He showed me the steps so that now I can.

On a bus, met a friend and with a smile,
I was talking to her across the aisle,
A passenger stood to change seats with me
So my friend and I could talk easily.

Home from a show, Playbill on my knee
Fellow riders will ask, "What did you see?"
"Oh, yes, I saw that performance too.
What would you give it in your review?"

On a bus, the man in the driver's seat,
Told me where I could find a particular street.
He joked, like a caring chaperone,
"Be sure to call me when you get home!"

It's not a secret! You can shout it.
Rudest City? Fuggetaboutit!

COMMUNICATION

Scene One: New York City bus,
Woman sitting near me
Talking on a cell phone
In a foreign language.
Second woman enters,
Sits next to cell phone user,
Who now completes her call.
Second Woman speaks
Animatedly to First Woman.
They laugh and talk
Until Second Woman leaves.
I think about how easily
You can begin
A friendly conversation
With a stranger on a bus
When you speak her language.

Scene Two: Third Woman on bus
Speaks to cell phone user,
"Were you speaking Farsi?"
"Yes, I was. That was clever of you
To recognize my language."

"I realized it was Farsi,"
 Says the Third Woman,
"Because I heard you say, 'Persia.'
Is it anything like Arabic?"
"No," Says the First Woman,
"Nothing like Arabic."
"Anything like Hebrew?"

"No," Says the First Woman.
"Nothing like Hebrew."
"It had lots of aitches,"
Says Woman number Three.
So it sounded like Hebrew."
They both leave at the next stop.

Scene Three: Fourth Woman, observing it all,
Looks at me and smiles.
"Have a nice day,"
She says to me in English.

SOUTHERN DISCOMFORT

Brought up in New York City,
But living in the South in the sixties,
I shocked the inhabitants,
By sitting down
At a drugstore counter
And ordering
A "black and white" ice cream soda.

TWO PROPOSALS

For two days in February the weather turned balmy
And I was involved in some daring adventures —
I received two proposals on two city buses.
I never imagined a bus was romantic.
It may be a case of early spring fever.

It began with a man on the crosstown bus.
"How are you doing? You look nice. Are you married?"
"A widow," I said. "I'd like to marry you," said he.
I said, "Your proposal is my first one today."
"Today!" he laughed. And I laughed too.

The next was a chat on the First Avenue bus
With a man revealed as "a tourist from Queens."
He said, "You're so nice, I'd like to take you home."
I smiled and replied, "I have a home, thank you."
I guess that he rode back to Queens by himself.

Maybe I should be a little more wary
But I have decided to look for adventure,
So I'm planning a bus trip on the next balmy day.

I HEAR A POEM

I hear a poem
Walking the noisy city streets:
Sirens screaming,
Bus horns blaring,
Trucks beeping a warning
Over and over, backing up,
Friends shouting to each other
Or talking on cell phones.

When on the edge of sleep
I listen to the city sounds
And am content. Life is out there,
The world is working as it should.
Before my visit to a quiet country town
I plan to tape the city sounds
To play when sleep eludes me,
So that I will feel safe and at home
Though I hear nothing but the owl's hoot.

NIGHT SOUNDS

Seaside
Through my open bedroom window:
    Crash of waves
    Squawk of gulls
    Moan of foghorns.

Countryside
A night lit only by stars:
    Hoot of owls
    Rustle of windswept trees
    Whistle of distant train.

City
Through the tightly closed casement:
    Scream of sirens
    Rumble of trucks
    People shouting, laughing.

Life.
Not better or worse...
    Simply different.

BRIEF ENCOUNTER

I wore my long gray designer coat
   (a hand-me down from my aunt,
   who gave it to my mother,
   who died 15 years ago).
I wore a white wool hat (crocheted
   by my cousin) and the velvet scarf
   (given to me by a dear friend
   for my birthday years ago).
I held a Bloomingdales bag
With clothes to be cleaned.
It was my birthday and I
Was going out to celebrate.
On first avenue, a young man
Walked toward me and demanded,
"Can I ask you a question?"
"I have an appointment," I said,
Trying to walk away.
"Do you respect me?" he asked, angrily,
Pointing his finger at me.
I saw that a gray-haired man had stopped
To watch what was happening.
Another curious New Yorker — I thought.
"What is your question?" I asked with a sigh.
"Can you give me money for a meal?"
Standing just behind me
The gray-haired man kept watching.
I opened my wallet. Found a twenty
Dollar bill and some change.
I offered the change. The man said,

"No! Do you respect me?"
The gray-haired man took my arm.
"There's an open stairwell behind you!"
He walked with me down First Avenue
To the door of the cleaning store.
I was shaken, from the angry encounter,
From a possible fall down basement stairs.
I thanked the gray-haired man,
And thought about perceptions.
Did I think the angry young man
Was asking directions?
Did the angry young man think
I was a rich East-sider
While he was poor and hungry?
   (He didn't know how old the coat was
   or that I was just bringing clothes
   to the cleaners in my Bloomingdales bag.)
Did I think the gray-haired man
Was a curious onlooker
When instead he was my savior?
Perceptions can fly in the face of truth.
Let me be warned.

FOOLISH THINGS
(for Arthur)

Self-published books where you were sole creator
Your favorite joke about a Jewish waiter

The reprint bought in an Old Lyme museum
City landmarks - how we love to see 'em

A ramekin of luscious creme brulee
A five-flight climb to see a classic play

A photograph of foggy mirror lake
Old movie films that kept us wide awake

Foolish things — but absolutely true —
And everything reminds me of you.

ECHOES

I'm drifting slowly from a nap
In his chair, book upon my lap,
I feel his presence as I wake.
I gaze at how our furniture was placed —
He measured twice to fit into the space
Without an inch to spare —
                      I can't erase
One moment of our story from my mind,
Nor leave any memories behind.
The echoes that I hear are not the kind
That frighten.
                They only make me know
That time without him simply goes too slow.
He's with me going anywhere I go.
Whispering confidently in my ear
"This is the route to take, the way is clear;
Down this street, and then a right turn here."
We laughed at the crazy world and at ourselves.
We told each other all there was to tell.
At the end he couldn't speak to say, "Farewell."

Every moment that we spent together
Echoes, and will stay with me forever.

The Following Poems Appeared Previously In
Q Review
The Creative Voice Of Quest

Advice For Troubled Times
A Polite Protest By A New Yorker
At The New York Philharmonic
Bagels And Romance
Echoes
Elephant Graveyard
Enchanted April
Dreams
I Don't Want To Move
Living Well
Southern Discomfort
State Fair
Surka's Stories

www.ingramcontent.com/pod-product-compliance
Lightning Source LLC
Chambersburg PA
CBHW050608300426
44112CB00013B/2121